Wat Phra Keo, The Temple Of The Emerald Buddha, In Bangkok

FACES
AND
PLACES

THAILAND

BY ALEX ERICSON

THE CHILD'S WORLD®, INC.

COVER PHOTO

A smiling boy near Mae San.
©Alison Wright/CORBIS

Published in the United States of America by The Child's World®, Inc.
PO Box 326
Chanhassen, MN 55317-0326
800-599-READ
www.childsworld.com

Project Manager James R. Rothaus/James R. Rothaus & Associates
Designer Robert E. Bonaker/R. E. Bonaker & Associates
Contributors Mary Berendes, Katherine Stevenson, Ph.D., Red Line Editorial

Library of Congress Cataloging-in-Publication Data
Ericson, Alex.
Thailand / by Alex Ericson.
p. cm.
Includes index.
ISBN 1-56766-913-1
1. Thailand—Juvenile Literature.
[1. Thailand]
I. Title.
DS563.5 .E74 2000
959.3—dc21

Table of Contents

Where Is Thailand?

Of all the planets in our solar system, only Earth has oceans full of water. Earth's oceans surround huge areas of land called **continents**. Thailand lies in the southeast part of the continent of Asia. Asia is the largest of Earth's seven continents.

Western Hemisphere

Eastern Hemisphere

Thailand (white) is in the east and U.S.A. (green) is in the west

Much of Thailand is nestled between the Southeast Asian countries of Myanmar (formerly called Burma),

The World Shown Flat

Laos, and Cambodia. Southern Thailand's long, skinny "tail" separates the Gulf of Thailand from the Andaman Sea. This part of Thailand is on the Malay **peninsula**, which is an area surrounded mostly by water and attached to land on only one side.

Arctic Ocean

NORTH AMERICA

United States of America

Atlantic Ocean

Pacific Ocean

SOUTH AMERICA

ASIA

EUROPE

AFRICA

Thailand

Indian Ocean

Pacific Ocean

AUSTRALIA

ANTARCTICA

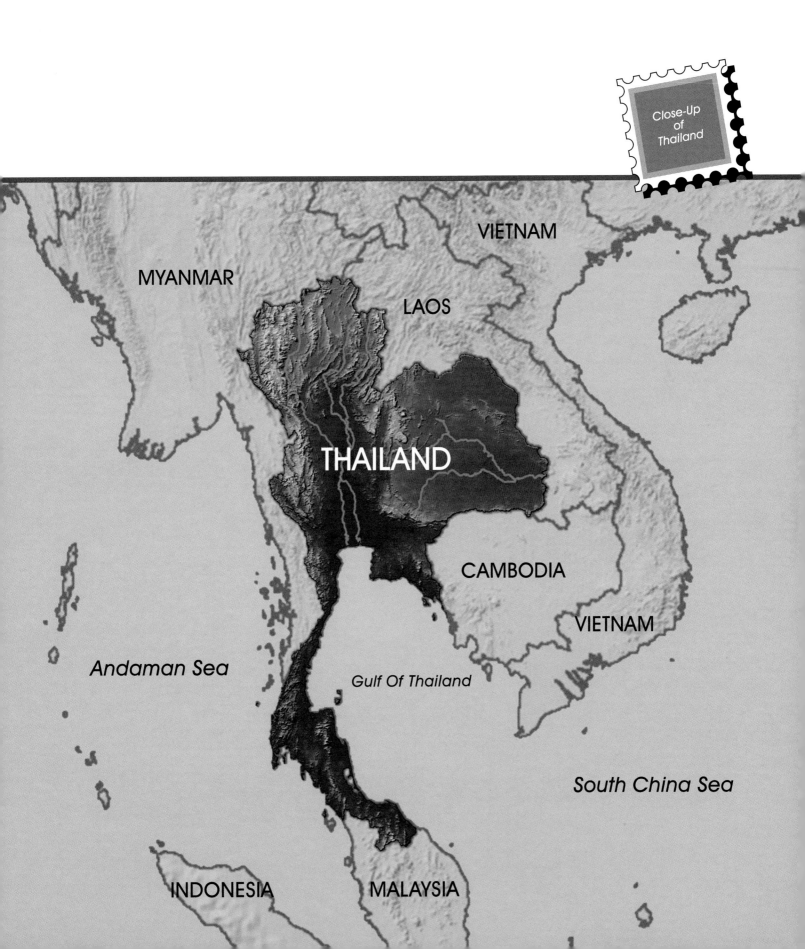

VIETNAM

MYANMAR

LAOS

THAILAND

CAMBODIA

VIETNAM

Andaman Sea

Gulf Of Thailand

South China Sea

INDONESIA

MALAYSIA

A Limestone Outcrop Near The Beach In Krabi

Mae Hong Son
Mae San
★ Bangkok
Krabi

©Eye Ubiquitous/CORBIS

The Land

Phi Ton Sai And Lodalum Bays On Phi Phi Don Island Near Krabi

Along its seacoast, southern Thailand has wonderful beaches and beautiful tropical islands. Much of southern Thailand is covered with thick tropical jungles, swamps, and forests. Northwestern Thailand has tall mountains with beautiful rivers and hidden valleys. There you can walk through forests and find waterfalls and caves.

©Eye Ubiquitous/CORBIS

Elephants Walking Up The Pai River

Most of Thailand, however, is a flat region with rivers and farmland. Many of these rivers flow into the Chao Phraya (JOW PRAH-YAH) river, which flows into the capital city of Bangkok. Other rivers in Thailand are so beautiful, many people spend a wonderful day simply sailing on the water.

©Kevin R. Morris/CORBIS

Asian Water Buffalo In A River Near A Jungle

©Ecoscene/CORBIS

Thailand's varied types of land support many different kinds of plants and animals. Throughout Thailand there are beautiful orchid flowers and a giant grass called **bamboo.** The mountains have huge forests of oak, teak, and evergreen trees. Southern Thailand has thick jungles of mangrove and palm trees.

Rice Paddies And Palm Trees North Of Bangkok

©Staffen Wdstrand/CORBIS

Thailand's forest regions are alive with animals such as crocodiles, giant snakes, bears, rhinos, tigers, and elephants. Thailand also has more kinds of birds than the entire continent of North America, despite its much smaller size. The waters off the southern peninsula are home to fish, sharks, and other sea creatures that live around coral reefs.

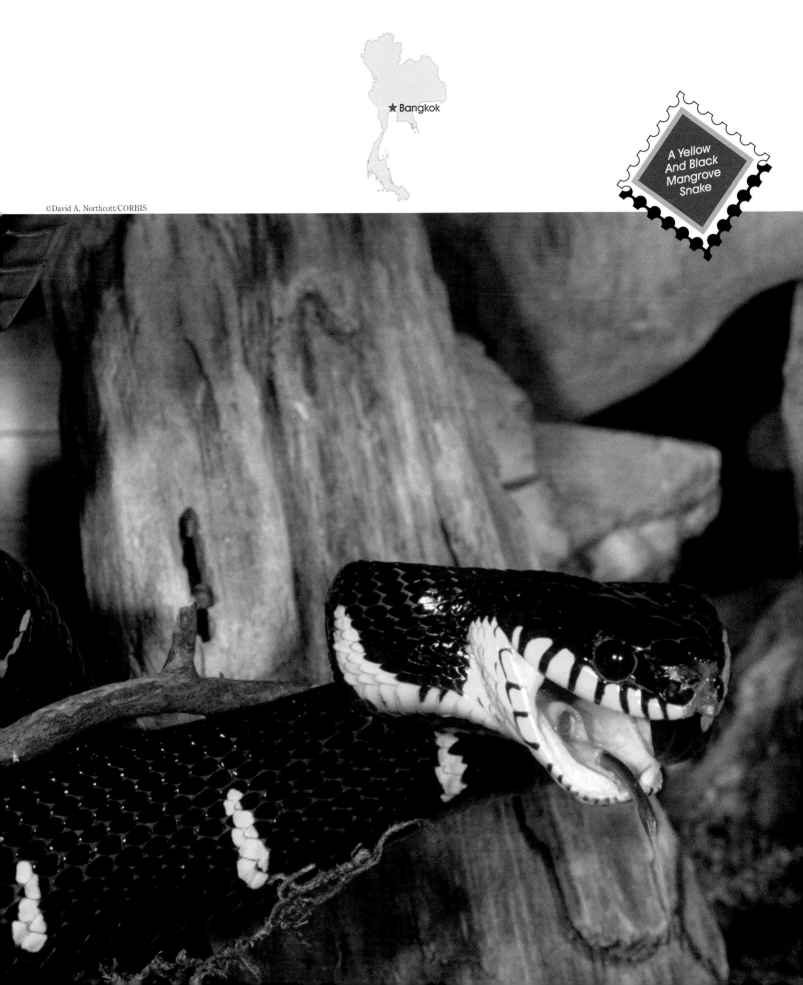

★Bangkok

©David A. Northcott/CORBIS

A Yellow
And Black
Mangrove
Snake

Ruins
Of Ancient
Temples
In
Ayutthaya

• Ayutthaya

An Old Thai Drawing Of A Royal Parade

People have lived in Thailand for thousands of years. The first known kingdom began 800 years ago. The kingdom was called *Sukhothai,* or "the dawn of happiness." During this time, much of Thailand's art and culture were developed. From the late 1800s until 1939, the nation was called *Siam.* Then its name was changed to Thailand, which means "land of the free."

The Gulf Of Siam In The 1800s

The history of Thailand is a history of its kings. For centuries the kings had almost total power. But in 1932, a **revolution** changed the country's form of government. The new government limited the power a Thai king could have. After that, the military had a major role in running the country.

Thailand Today

Thailand still has a king, but he has little direct power. Today the military has less power, too. Instead, Thailand has a prime minister and a **legislature** made up of a House of Representatives and a Senate. The legislature is elected by the people and makes the nation's laws. All Thai people age 18 and over can vote to elect these leaders.

Just like its government, Thailand is a mixture of old and new. Big new skyscrapers stand near ancient temples. People in cities drive cars to work, while people in villages use elephants to help them work. Today, Thailand is trying hard to develop new technology while keeping its old traditions.

King Rama IX And Queen Sirkit In Hat Yai

A Barge Traveling Along The Chao Phraya River In Bangkok

★ Bangkok

● Hat Yai

©Paul Almasy/CORBIS

• Mae Hong Son

A Lisu Girl Carrying Wood In North Thailand

©Papilo/CORBIS

Thailand is heavily populated, and its population is still growing. In fact, one-fourth of Thailand's people are children. Seven out of every ten Thai people have the same cultural or **ethnic** background.

Religion is of great importance to the Thai people. Almost everyone in Thailand is **Buddhist**, or a follower of the teachings of Buddha. Buddhism is a belief that every action or thought has a **consequence**. Buddhists also believe that people can reach a state of "enlightenment," or wisdom, by trying to do good things. Almost every town in Thailand has a *wat,* or temple, and Buddhist monks in orange robes.

A Karen Woman With Neck Extension Rings In Mae Hong Son

©Nik Wheeler/CORBIS

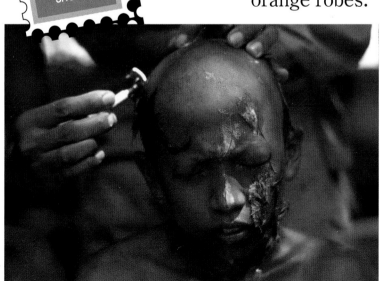

A Young Monk Getting His Head Shaved

©Eye Ubiquitous/CORBIS

Thai people treat older people with great respect. From the elderly, the young learn to be polite and accepting of others. Thailand's people are known for being warm and friendly.

City Life And Country Life

A Man Poling A Boat In A River Near Ubon Ratchathani

©Roman Soumar/CORBIS

About 80 percent of Thailand's people live in the country. They live on small farms or in villages. In the villages, grandparents, uncles, aunts, and many relatives all live close to each other. Some ways of country life are much like they were long ago. For example, instead of fancy machines, elephants are sometimes used to work in the forests and mountains. These animals are trained to help move heavy items or carry people from place to place.

Thailand also has many large cities. With a population of well over 5 million people, Bangkok is the largest city in Thailand. Life in Bangkok is like life in most large cities. There are busy roads, tall buildings, shops, restaurants, and even zoos.

A Bangkok Policeman Directing Traffic

©Charles E. Rotkin/CORBIS

Ubon Ratchathani •
★ Bangkok

©Paul Almasy/CORBIS

An Elephant Using Its Trunk To Move Logs

A Page From An Old Thai Book

©Luca I. Tettoni/CORBIS

In Thailand, all children are required to go to elementary school from ages 6 to 12. They study reading, writing, and math just as you do. Almost all Thai children go to school until they are 14, but few go on to higher education.

A Crowd Of Schoolboys Sitting In A Schoolyard

Eye Ubiquitous/CORBIS

The official language of Thailand is Thai. Words in Thai mean different things depending on how the words are said. A single Thai word can have different meanings depending on whether it is said with a high, low, or even tone.

A Coffee Picker In Mae San

In the country, most Thai people are farmers. The most important crop in Thailand is rice. To grow rice, farmers must keep the field, or **paddy**, wet. Often, rice paddies are completely under water. Farmers also grow bananas, pineapples, and many other crops. Besides farming, Thai people also mine for minerals, harvest wood for building and fuel, and catch seafood to eat and sell.

Fishermen In Phangnga Bay

In the city, people work in restaurants, shops, and factories. Thai factories make everything from clothes to computers. Thailand's beautiful silk cloths are especially well known. There are many different jobs in Thailand!

Mae San

★ Bangkok

PHANGNGA BAY

Young Men Painting Parasols In Bangkok

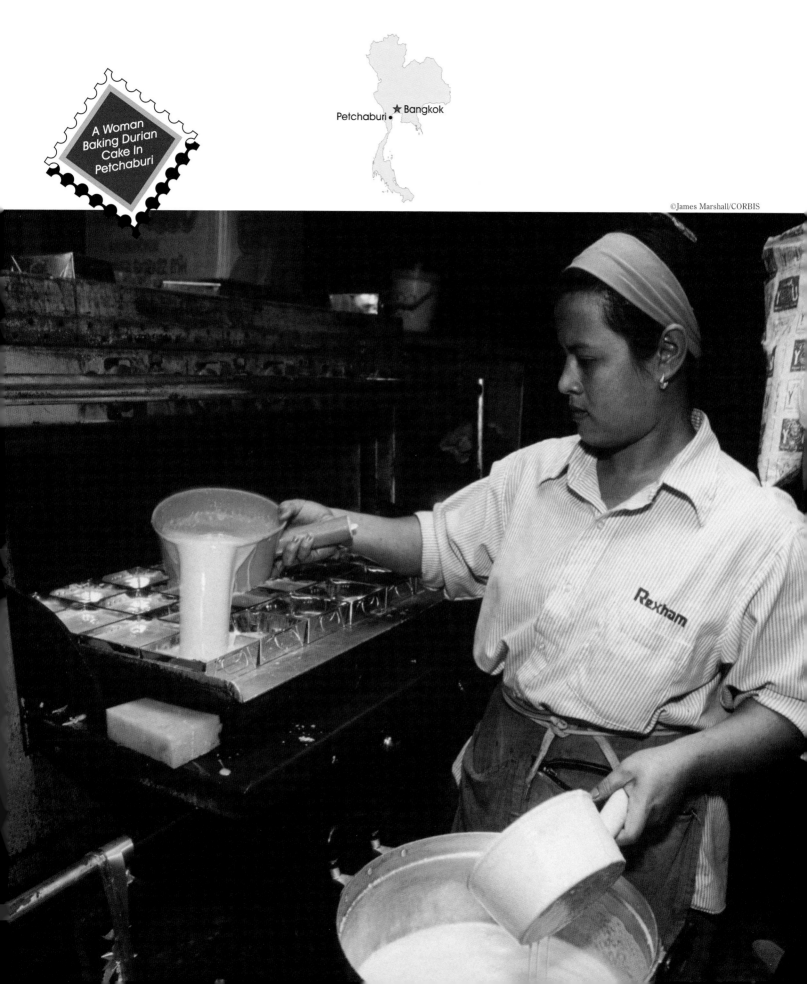

A Woman Baking Durian Cake In Petchaburi

Petchaburi • ★ Bangkok

Food

Thai food is as pleasing to the eye as it is to the taste buds. All the dishes in a Thai meal are served at once so that you can taste and see all the different combinations. A meal might include a rice dish, soups, a curry dish, a vegetable or fish dish, spicy salads, a sweet fruit dessert, and plenty of dips and sauces.

Fruit Merchants At Bangkok's Floating Market

©Keren Su/CORBIS

A Scorpion-and-Noodle Dish In Bangkok

©Owen Franken/CORBIS

Thai people love to use lots of spices and seasonings in their food. Curry, garlic, and ginger are common spices in Thai dishes. Many people also enjoy sauces with their meals, especially *nam plaa.* This favorite fish sauce is used in many recipes.

25

Pastimes and Holidays

Thai people try to find *sanuk,* or enjoyment, in everything they do, from visiting with friends to enjoying the night air. Sports are popular, including familiar sports such as soccer, golf, and tennis. Thailand has its own traditional sports, too. In Thai kite flying, teams use fancy kites to capture or knock down each other's kites. In the popular sport of Thai boxing, the boxers use their feet, legs, elbows, or fists to knock down their opponent.

Thailand has many holidays and festivals, and most of them are religious. Many of them also celebrate important times in the Thai calendar, such as the king's birthday or the new year. Holidays are times for singing, dancing, food, and fireworks.

Thailand is a country with something for everyone. You can find loud parades and fun parties, or quiet walks and beautiful scenery. From the beaches to the mountains, a trip to Thailand is sure to be an adventure you'll always remember!

A Boy Flying A Kite In Bangkok

©Kevin R. Morris/CORBIS

Chiang Mai

Nakhon Pathom • Nakhon Ratchasima

★ Bangkok

Petchaburi •

Nakhon Si Thammarat

Songkhla

©Kevin R. Morris/CORBIS

Temple Dancers Performing A Lakom Dance In Bangkok

Area
About 198,000 square miles
(514,000 square kilometers)—almost three times as big as Washington state.

Population
About 60 million people.

Capital City
Bangkok.

Other Important Cities
Chiang Mai, Songkhla, Nakhon Si Thammarat, and Nakhon Ratchasima.

Money
The baht, which is divided into 100 satang.

National Song
"Phleng Chat," or "National Anthem."

National Holiday
The king's birthday on December 5.

National Flag
The flag has five stripes. The top and bottom stripes are red, the next two are white, and the middle stripe is blue. The red stands for Thailand. The white represents religion. The blue stripe is meant to show respect for the king.

Official Name
The Kingdom of Thailand.

Heads of Government
The prime minister and the king of Thailand.

Thailand Trivia

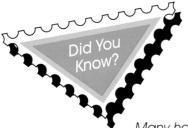

Did You Know?

Many houses in Thai villages are built on poles to avoid frequent floods.

Because of its wonderful weather, Thailand has many different types of fruit. Some, like bananas and pineapples, are common. More unusual Thai fruits have names like durian, rambutan, magostee, logans, and lychee. The durian fruit is famous for its terrible smell—like something that's rotten. Durians are sometimes banned from public areas because they smell so bad!

The city of Nakhon Pathom is home to the tallest Buddhist monument in the world. This monument, called the Phra Pathom Chedi, is over 400 feet tall.

Religion is so important in Thailand that many boys and men spend part of their lives as Buddhist monks.

Thailand has some of the longest family names in the world. Many of them belong to families who moved to Thailand from China. When the newcomers applied to the government for new Thai names, they had to make up names no other family had used before. As more and more people applied for new names, the names kept getting longer and longer.

How Do You Say?

	THAI	HOW TO SAY IT
Hello	sa–wat–dee	SOW–WAH–DEE
Good-bye	lar–korn	LAR–korn
Please	ka–ru–na	kah–ROO–nah
Thank You	kob–khun	kob–KOON
One	neung	NOONG
Two	sorng	SOHRNG
Three	sarm	SAHRM
Thailand	Thailand	TY–land

bamboo (bam-BOO)
Bamboo is a tall, thick grass that grows in warm, wet parts of the world. Bamboo grows in many parts of Thailand.

Buddhist (BOOD-hist)
A Buddhist is a person who follows the religion of Buddhism. Almost all of Thailand's people are Buddhists.

consequence (KON-seh-kwenss)
A consequence is a result of a person's actions. Buddhists believe every action or thought has a consequence.

continents (KON-tih-nents)
A continent is one of Earth's seven large land masses. Thailand is in the southeastern part of the huge continent of Asia.

ethnic (ETH-nik)
Ethnic means belonging to a certain group or type of people. Most of Thailand's people come from the same ethnic background.

legislature (LEJ-ih-slay-chur)
A legislature is a group of people who make laws for a country. Thailand has a legislature.

paddy (PAD-dee)
A paddy is a flooded field used to grow rice. Thailand has many rice paddies.

peninsula (peh-NIN-suh-luh)
A peninsula is an area of land that is attached to a larger land area and has water almost all the way around it. Southern Thailand is on a peninsula.

revolution (reh-vuh-LOO-shun)
A revolution is a sudden or violent uprising to change a nation's government. Thailand had a revolution in 1932.

Index

Web Sites

Learn more about Thailand:
http://www.pbs.org/edens/thailand/
http://lcweb2.loc.gov/frd/cs/thtoc.html
http://www.thaiembdc.org/
http://www.lonelyplanet.com/destinations/south_east_asia/thailand/

Listen to Thailand's national anthem:
http://www.emulateme.com/thailand.htm

Learn how to say more words in Thai:
http://www.travlang.com/languages/
(Then be sure to click on the word "Thai.")

Find recipes for many different Thai dishes:
http://www.tat.or.th/food/index.htm